# ANIMALS AT RISK
# PANDAS IN DANGER

## BY MICHAEL PORTMAN

**Gareth Stevens**
Publishing

Please visit our website, www.garethstevens.com. For a free color catalog of all our high-quality books, call toll free 1-800-542-2595 or fax 1-877-542-2596.

**Library of Congress Cataloging-in-Publication Data**

Portman, Michael, 1976-
Pandas in danger / Michael Portman.
    p. cm. — (Animals at risk)
Includes index.
ISBN 978-1-4339-5800-7 (pbk.)
ISBN 978-1-4339-5801-4 (6-pack)
ISBN 978-1-4339-5798-7 (library binding)
1. Giant panda—Juvenile literature. 2. Endangered species—Juvenile literature. I. Title.
QL737.C27P676 2011
333.95'9789—dc22

                                   2010053764

First Edition

Published in 2012 by
**Gareth Stevens Publishing**
111 East 14th Street, Suite 349
New York, NY 10003

Copyright © 2012 Gareth Stevens Publishing

Designer: Haley W. Harasymiw
Editor: Therese M. Shea

Photo credits: Cover, pp. 1, 5, 7, 9, 10, 11, 13, 14, 15, 17, 19, 20 Shutterstock.com.

Printed in the United States of America

CPSIA Compliance Information: Batch #CR216260GS: For further information contact Gareth Stevens, New York, New York at 1-800-542-2595.

# CONTENTS

Words in the glossary appear in **bold** type the first time they are used in the text.

# PEACEFUL PANDAS

The giant panda is one of the most loved animals in the world. It's also one of the most **endangered** animals. These black-and-white bears were once found throughout the countries of Myanmar (also called Burma), Vietnam, and China. Today, giant pandas only live high in the mountains of China.

Giant pandas are peaceful. They have very few enemies in nature, yet they face many dangers. Their main **threats** are loss of their homes, food shortages, few babies, and illegal hunting.

Though pandas are bears, they don't roar. Instead, they make a sound like a goat or lamb makes.

## WILD FACTS

For many years, scientists weren't sure if giant pandas were a type of bear or raccoon, or their own kind of animal.

Giant pandas live in cool, rainy bamboo forests in the mountains of central China. "Bamboo" is the name for a family of giant, tree-like grasses. These grasses are the panda's main food source. Bamboo doesn't have many **nutrients**, so pandas must eat a lot of it to stay healthy. Each day, they spend about 12 hours eating.

Bamboo provides the pandas with most of the water they need. However, they must still drink freshwater from streams and rivers every day.

## WILD FACTS
A giant panda eats about 30 pounds (14 kg) of bamboo a day. It sometimes eats other plants and even small birds and **rodents**.

Pandas have paws that are perfect for holding bamboo stems while they chomp.

# BLOOMING BAMBOO

Like other plants, bamboo blooms and produces seeds. Then it dies. For each type of bamboo, all the plants bloom and die at the same time. It can take up to 10 years for the seeds to grow into bamboo that's ready to be eaten by the pandas. Luckily for the pandas, more than one kind of bamboo usually grows in an area. When one kind dies, giant pandas eat another kind or move to another area if they can.

▼ Pandas eat about 25 kinds of bamboo.

**WILD FACTS**

Bamboo plants bloom every 30 to 120 years, depending on the kind.

9

# A Changing Habitat

In the past, giant pandas could easily move to find more food. Sadly, it's now hard for pandas to travel throughout their **habitat**. This is because China has the largest population in the world. More than 1 billion people live there. Over many years, large sections of the giant panda's habitat were cleared for farms and for wood. In addition, roads were built through the forests. Giant pandas were cut off from each other and from other areas of food.

The process of clearing forest areas is called deforestation.

# FOREST ISLANDS

In the 1970s and 1980s, giant pandas lost about half of their habitat. Now, they live in about 20 small areas of mountainous forest. These areas are forest "islands," separated by large spaces of cleared land. Giant pandas won't **migrate** between these islands to search for new food. If not enough bamboo grows in the pandas' area, they can die of hunger. Today, there may be as few as 1,600 giant pandas in the wild.

## WILD FACTS

There are about 100 to 300 giant pandas living in zoos. Much of what we know about giant pandas comes from studying them in zoos.

▼ Giant pandas don't sleep through winter like some other bears. They need to keep eating!

# Mates and Cubs

Habitat loss has made it hard for giant pandas to **reproduce**. Giant pandas spend most of their time alone or in small groups. They come together to choose a **mate**. However, it's harder for them to find a mate in their separate forest islands.

Female giant pandas give birth to one or two cubs at a time. Usually, only one cub lives. Mother pandas raise just five to eight cubs in their lifetime. This means it takes a long time for the giant panda population to grow.

**WILD FACTS**

Newborn giant panda cubs are about the size of a stick of butter. They're born blind and hairless.

▼ Giant panda cubs begin to climb trees when they're about 6 months old.

# DEADLY TRAPS

Giant pandas also face the threat of illegal hunting, or poaching. Poachers sell the meat of wild animals to markets in China. They don't usually mean to hunt giant pandas. However, the pandas can get caught in traps that were meant for other animals. These traps can seriously hurt or even kill them.

In the past, giant pandas were hunted for their fur or to sell to zoos. Today, China has very strict laws against hunting giant pandas.

▼ Young giant pandas are popular animals in zoos because they're so playful.

17

The Chinese government is working with **conservation** groups to keep giant pandas and their habitat safe. Over 50 **nature reserves** were created in order to guard giant pandas from the threats of deforestation and poaching.

The Chinese government and conservation groups are also working to connect forest islands with **corridors** of bamboo. These corridors make it possible for giant pandas to travel to other parts of the forest to find food and to meet mates.

**WILD FACTS**

Giant pandas can live over 20 years in the wild and over 30 years in zoos.

Pandas' black-and-white markings help them blend in with their forest habitat.

# Hope for the Future

Scientists continue to study giant pandas. They hope to learn more about how the animals talk to each other and how to keep them healthy.

Thanks to conservation efforts, the giant panda population seems to be growing. However, nature reserves cover less than half of the giant panda habitat. This includes about 60 percent of the panda population. Giant pandas need more help from people around the world. There is still hope for these beautiful animals.

## How Big Are Giant Pandas?

| | |
|---|---|
| Length | 4 to 5 feet (1.2 to 1.5 m) |
| Height | 27 to 32 inches (69 to 81 cm) |
| Weight | 220 to 330 pounds (100 to 150 kg) |

# GLOSSARY

**conservation:** the care of the natural world

**corridor:** a strip of land

**endangered:** in danger of dying out

**habitat:** an area where plants, animals, or other living things live

**mate:** one of two animals that come together to produce babies

**migrate:** to travel from one habitat to another

**nature reserve:** a safe area for endangered animals

**nutrient:** something in food that helps a living thing stay healthy

**reproduce:** when plants or animals create new plants or animals

**rodent:** a small animal with large teeth, such as a mouse or rat

**threat:** something likely to cause harm

# FOR MORE INFORMATION

## BOOKS

Greve, Tom. *Giant Pandas.* Vero Beach, FL: Rourke Publishing, 2011.

Schreiber, Anne. *Pandas.* Washington, DC: National Geographic, 2010.

## WEBSITES

**Giant Panda**
www.worldwildlife.org/species/finder/giantpanda/panda.html
Read about conservation efforts to help giant pandas.

**Mammals: Giant Panda**
www.sandiegozoo.org/animalbytes/t-giant_panda.html
Read fun facts about giant pandas.

**Panda Cam**
www.zooatlanta.org/1212/panda_cam
See pictures and live video of the baby panda at the Atlanta Zoo.

# INDEX